白
蛇
傳

For Anne
– *A. S.*

In memory of my father, Zhang Can (1903–2000), who was
born in the Fuyang district of Hangzhou
– *S. N. Z.*

LADY
White Snake

白
蛇
傳

Published in the United States of America by
Pan Asian Publications (USA) Inc.
29564 Union City Boulevard, Union City, California 94587
Tel. (510) 475-1185 Fax (510) 475-1489

Published in Canada by
Pan Asian Publications Inc.
110 Silver Star Boulevard, Unit 109
Scarborough, Ontario M1V-5A2

ISBN 1-57227-072-1
Library of Congress Catalog Card Number: 2001 086179

Design by Lorna Mulligan
Art reproduction and transparencies by Michel Filion Photography
Editorial and production assistance: William Mersereau,
Art & Publishing Consultants

Printed in Hong Kong by the South China Printing Co. Ltd.

LADY White Snake

A TALE FROM CHINESE OPERA

Retold by Aaron Shepard   Illustrated by Song Nan Zhang

Pan Asian Publications

How to say the names:

These pronunciations are very approximate and can vary from region to region within China.

Emei	um-AY
Fahai	FAH-HI
Hangzhou	HONG-JO
Kunlun	KUN-LUN
Xu Xian	SOO see-EN *or* SHOO shee-EN
Yangzi	YONG-dzuh
Zhenjiang	JUN-jee-ONG

About the Chinese title calligraphy:

For the title and subtitle of this book, the artist Mr. Zhang has adapted an ancient style of Chinese calligraphy (ornamental writing) called Zhuàn (JOO-on), or "seal" calligraphy. Stone, ivory and wooden seals, or 'chops,' have been used for over 2,000 years to stamp formal signatures of people or organizations onto documents, usually in red ink. Note that the Chinese characters must be carved backwards for them to appear properly on paper. It is interesting to compare the differences in the three ancient Zhuàn style characters for Lady White Snake with the present-day Chinese.

白 **BÁI** white

蛇 **SHÉ** snake

傳 **CHUÁN** legend

A tale from Chinese opera:

經 **JĪNG** classic stories

XÌ theatrical play 戲

典 **DIǍN** typical classics

QŪ singing opera 曲

The old tales of China tell us that all things may grow and change. A stone may become a plant. A plant may become an animal. An animal may become a human. A human may become a god.

Just so, a snake may become a woman. And we are told of one who did.

Who can say for sure how it began? Yet after centuries of ceaseless effort—meditating, disciplining herself, mastering the energies of the universe—this white snake took human form. Immortal now and with great powers, she longed for one thing more.

Human love.

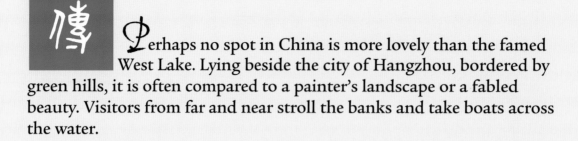

$\mathcal{P}$erhaps no spot in China is more lovely than the famed West Lake. Lying beside the city of Hangzhou, bordered by green hills, it is often compared to a painter's landscape or a fabled beauty. Visitors from far and near stroll the banks and take boats across the water.

Among the strollers on one spring day long ago was a lovely young lady dressed in white and her young maid in blue—or so they seemed. How could anyone know they were really a white snake and a blue snake in human form? Flying on clouds from their home on sacred Mount Emei, they had come to Hangzhou to sample the joys of the human world.

"It's even more beautiful than I'd hoped," said Lady White as they walked along. "Can you smell the peach blossoms? And look, Blue! Here's the famous Broken Bridge."

"But the bridge isn't broken!" said Blue.

"That's just what it's called," said Lady White, smiling. "Oh, sister, I'm so glad we came here from our cold and dreary mountain."

As the sun passed behind dark clouds, they spotted a young man with an umbrella under his arm. "How handsome he is!" said Blue, and Lady White agreed. Her heart felt something she had never known before.

Just then it began to rain, and they took shelter under a willow. The young man, whose name was Xu Xian, noticed their predicament. "Ladies," he said, "that willow won't keep you dry! Please use my umbrella."

"But, sir, you need it yourself," said Lady White.

"Don't worry about me," he said. "Look, there's a boat coming to shore. Let me hire the boatman to take us back to the city."

As they crossed the lake, the ladies insisted that the young man sit close to share the umbrella. He and Lady White exchanged shy glances and spoke awkwardly, while Blue helped the conversation along and smiled in amused delight.

Before long, the boat reached the landing the ladies had asked for. By then the rain had stopped, but Blue pointed secretly skyward, and it started once again.

Just as hoped, the young man said, "Please, you must take the umbrella home with you. I'll come for it tomorrow."

"Thank you, sir," said Lady White. "We will expect you. Please do not disappoint us!"

The next morning, Xu Xian visited the house where the ladies were staying. As Blue served tea and then wine, the young man told Lady White he was an orphan and had been returning from a visit to his mother's grave when he met them. He lived with his sister and her husband and worked as an assistant in a shop for herbal medicine.

Pleased by his words and his manner, Lady White whispered to Blue and left the room. Blue said, "My mistress wants to know if you would like to marry her."

In surprise, the young man said, "There's nothing I'd like better! But with the little I earn, how could I support the three of us?"

"Oh, don't worry about that," said Blue. "My mistress has an inheritance from her father. Anyway, today is lucky, so you really should get married right away. You can tell your sister later, and that umbrella will do just fine as a gift for the bride. I'll light the candles, and everything will be ready."

Almost before he knew it, Xu Xian was standing next to Lady White in her bridal gown. They bowed to Heaven and Earth, to their ancestors, and to each other. They were now husband and wife!

The newlyweds decided to move to the city of Zhenjiang and open an herb shop of their own. The shop was a great success, for Lady White could tell just what was wrong with a patient and just what compound to prescribe. What's more, she showed great dedication in helping the sick, no matter how poor.

The two were supremely happy with their work and with each other. Adding to their joy, Lady White soon announced she was expecting a child.

One day, when Lady White had gone off to rest, an old Buddhist monk entered the shop and spoke to Xu Xian. "I am Fahai, the abbot of Gold Mountain Temple," he said. "I have come to warn you of a great danger. By my spiritual powers, I have discovered that your wife is a thousand-year-old snake. She hides her true nature for now, but one day she will surely turn on you and devour you."

"How dare you say that!" said the young man. "It's nothing but wicked slander!"

But Fahai told him, "If you don't believe it, just make sure she drinks realgar wine for the Dragon Boat Festival. She'll then change back to her true form, and you'll see for yourself."

Soon came the Dragon Boat Festival, when everyone drank wine mixed with foul-smelling realgar to drive away snakes. Knowing the danger to her kind, Lady White stayed in bed pretending to be ill. But Xu Xian called her out of the bedroom and said cheerily, "We mustn't let the festival pass without sharing at least one cup of realgar wine!"

When his wife made excuses, he suddenly remembered Fahai's warning and mentioned it as a joke. Lady White was horrified at this unexpected attack on their happiness. Afraid then to make her husband suspicious, and hoping by her powers to withstand the realgar, she drank one cup and then another.

Before she could drink a third, she began to retch. She quickly returned to the bedroom, while Xu Xian hurried out to prepare her some medicine. But when he came back with it, he found on the bed not his lovely wife but a huge white snake.

The young man collapsed to the floor, where Blue found him moments later. "Sister," she called, "wake up! Your husband has died of shock!"

Lady White, again in human form, knelt by her husband and wept. Then she declared, "I will fly to Kunlun Mountain and steal a miracle mushroom from the gods. That and nothing else can bring him back to life."

Taking both her own sword and Blue's, Lady White flew swiftly on a cloud all the way to holy Kunlun Mountain. But just as she came upon one of the miracle mushrooms, she was challenged by Brown Deer, a guard serving the gods. "I beg you," said Lady White, "spare one mushroom to save my husband's life."

"These mushrooms are not for mortals!" said Brown Deer.

He struck at her with his sword, but she met it with her own. "Then forgive me if I take one anyway," she said. And she fought back until she wounded him.

Lady White picked the mushroom and turned to flee. But just then White Crane, another guard, joined the fight. With a sword in each hand, Lady White defended herself bravely. But she was no match for both guards together and was finally beaten to the ground.

As White Crane raised his sword for a final blow, the Old Man of the South appeared and called a halt. "How dare you steal from us!" the god demanded of Lady White. But he could not help admiring her devotion to her husband. For that and the child she was expecting, he pardoned her and let her take the mushroom away.

With a drink made from the miracle mushroom, Lady White brought her husband back to life. But though he soon recovered fully, neither one of them would speak of what had happened. Terrified by what he had seen, and not knowing of his wife's efforts to save him, Xu Xian now did his best to avoid her.

Lady White, anxious to regain his love, at last played a trick on him. She changed her white silk sash into a living snake and fooled him into thinking that this was the snake that had frightened him.

Happiness returned to the household. But not long after, Xu Xian set off for Gold Mountain Temple to offer thanks to Buddha for his recovery. On the bank of the Yangzi River, he found Fahai waiting for him. "Your wife has tricked you," said Fahai, and he told him just what had happened.

Terrified once more, the young man asked, "How can I save myself?"

"Become a monk and live at the temple," said Fahai. "That's the one place she can't reach you."

But Xu Xian, torn between love of his wife and fear of her, could not decide. "I stand in two boats at once!" he moaned. At last, meaning to decide later, he boarded Fahai's raft and crossed with him to the river island where the temple stood.

Once inside Gold Mountain Temple, Xu Xian was not allowed to leave. Meanwhile, Lady White waited anxiously without news for three days. Then she and Blue took their swords and rowed a boat to the island to bring him home.

Fahai was there waiting for them. Blue cried, "Give him back, you shaven-headed donkey!" But Lady White silenced her. Patiently appealing to Fahai's compassion and sense of justice, she pleaded with him to return her husband.

"Demon!" cried Fahai. "My duty is to protect unsuspecting humans from such as you!"

"I have harmed no one and helped many," protested Lady White. "Surely the demon is he who divides man and wife!"

"Sister," declared Blue, "we must crush this temple!"

Fahai called down an army of heavenly warriors, while from the river below, Lady White and Blue called up an army of water animals. The two armies fought fiercely, and led by Lady White, her side was winning. But at last her condition made her falter. With her allies around her for protection, she hastily retreated.

$\mathcal{L}$ady White and Blue fled to Hangzhou, where they found themselves once more by Broken Bridge. Believing her husband had betrayed her. Lady White said, "The bridge may not be broken, but my heart is."

Blue told her, "If I ever see that traitor again, I'll kill him!"

Just then, Xu Xian himself arrived. From within the temple, he had heard the noise of battle and learned it was his wife who had come for him. Determined at last to stand by her, he had managed to escape, then had searched till he found them.

But Blue, furious at sight of him, chased him with her sword. Lady White stood between them to protect her husband, but then turned on him herself and declared how he had hurt her. The young man protested, "Fahai kept me prisoner—yet all that time I only thought of you!"

"Dear husband," said Lady White, "set aside your fear and hear me now." Then, ignoring Blue's signals of alarm, she revealed everything—what she was in truth and all she had done for him. "And now," she said, "your heart must tell you what is right or wrong."

Xu Xian replied, "Finally I realize all you've suffered for my sake. Human or not, I'll love you always. If I don't, let Blue cut off my head!"

United once more, the three stayed in Hangzhou with the sister of Xu Xian, and there Lady White gave birth to her baby boy. But the couple's happiness was not to last. Just one month after their son's birth—on the day they were to present him to friends and relatives—Fahai arrived, his golden alms bowl carried by a heavenly warrior. Lady White was instantly held captive by the bowl's golden ray.

Blue attacked the warrior with her sword, but he fought her off with Fahai's dragon staff. "Sister, save yourself," called Lady White, "and come back later to avenge us!" Helpless for the moment, Blue fled.

Xu Xian pleaded with Fahai and tried to seize the bowl, but to no avail. "Now at last," he said, "I see who is the real demon!"

Realizing there was no hope, Lady White said goodbye to her husband and to her baby. Then she told Fahai, "Though you tear me from my husband's arms, you cannot stop our love."

Then Fahai ordered the warrior to imprison her under Thunder Peak Pagoda by West Lake. He declared, "Not until the lake dries up or the pagoda falls will she come out again!"

*C*enturies passed. Xu Xian and Fahai passed away, but Blue did not forget. On Mount Emei, she trained herself until her powers were at their height. Then she gathered an army of mountain animals and marched on Thunder Peak Pagoda.

The pagoda's guardian spirit met her with his own army, but it was defeated and forced to flee. Then Blue's army set fire to the pagoda, which quickly crumbled.

"Sister, come out!" called Blue.

And there from the ruins rose Lady White—free again at last!

So ends the legend of Lady White. Who can say for sure what happened then? Perhaps she returned to Mount Emei, never more to brave the human world. Perhaps she flew above the clouds to live in peace in Heaven.

Or perhaps she strolls beside West Lake along with sister Blue, waiting for her heart to stir again.

A Guide to Lady White Snake

To help you enjoy and understand *Lady White Snake*, here are some notes on Chinese opera and on the story itself. For more resources, please visit my Web page at **www.aaronshep.com.**

About Chinese Opera

Imagine you are sitting in a theater, listening to a heroine sing longingly of her beloved. Suddenly the stage is invaded by two bands of acrobatic warriors. They tumble and twirl, cartwheel and somersault, flip this way and that. From the orchestra come sounds of cymbal, gong, and clapper to punctuate the action.

Swords clash, and warriors duck and dodge the blades. Spears fly, only to be hit or kicked back to the thrower—one, two, even four at a time. And what's this? The heroine has grabbed a sword to join the fight!

Welcome to the world of Chinese opera.

Actually, the word "opera" only begins to describe this pinnacle of China's traditional performing arts. Like opera in Western countries, Chinese opera features acting, singing, and sumptuous costumes. But it also offers dance, mime, face painting, and acrobatics.

Chinese opera evolved from the earliest Chinese dramas in the twelfth century. Over time, various stage arts were added and integrated until Chinese opera emerged as the country's most popular entertainment. In the nineteenth and early twentieth centuries, acclaimed opera actors were China's superstars.

But Chinese opera suffered gravely during China's Cultural Revolution (1966-1976), when it was almost completely banned, and since then has found itself eclipsed by modern forms of entertainment. Still, it survives today as a "classical" art, honored and appreciated for its place in China's traditional culture, as well as enjoyed for itself.

Chinese opera is a tradition with many branches. The best-known is Beijing Opera (or Peking Opera, in the older spelling) performed throughout China as well as overseas. But there are also over 300 regional operas, much alike in stage technique, costume, and stories performed, but differing in music and dialect.

Here is a look at some key aspects of Chinese opera.

The stories

There are over 1200 stories used in Chinese opera, mostly drawn from historical legend and mythology. Many promote traditional Chinese values like respect for parents, female modesty, and obedience to authority, while others encourage resistance to injustice or show women in unusually strong roles. For example, female generals are much more common in Chinese opera than in Chinese history.

At least until modern times, audiences were already familiar with the stories they saw performed, so they did not need to see an opera from beginning to end to understand it. For this reason, a traditional performance might be made up only of favorite scenes from one or more operas.

The characters

Each character in a Chinese opera is based on a standard role type, which is recognized at a glance by costume, makeup, and demeanor. This lets the audience know much about a character from the moment the actor comes onstage.

Among the female role types are the young lady, the lively girl, the refined woman, the older woman, and the military woman. Male role types include the young man, the older man, and the military man.

A special group of role types is the "painted faces"—male characters whose strong and simple personalities are represented by mask-like face painting. This group can include heroes, villains, generals, gods, and demons. (For more about them, see the section below on makeup.) Another special group is the clowns, both male and female, who provide humor through foolishness or wit.

The actors

An actor in Chinese opera is trained especially for one role type and will generally stick to it throughout his or her career. The choice is based on body type and abilities rather than age. For instance, a young male actor might always portray older men.

Until modern times, it was illegal in China for males and females to perform together. So, just as in Shakespeare's England, female roles were performed by men, who imitated female movements and sang falsetto. Today female roles are almost always played by females, but actresses still copy the voice and movement styles of their male predecessors.

Because of the many skills and the physical agility needed by opera actors, training must begin in childhood. Special schools in China offer this training along with general education.

The stage

The oldest form of the Chinese opera stage is a square platform of bamboo and planks, with the audience on three sides. Corner poles hold a canopy overhead, while a rug or mats cover the floor. An embroidered curtain stretches across the back, with two flaps for the actors to enter and exit. There is no curtain in front, no scenery, and no large props besides a table and chairs.

This kind of stage was designed to be portable, so an opera company could assemble it quickly in a public square or wherever else needed. Permanent opera stages were sometimes built in teahouses, palaces, and temple courtyards, but the basic design was the same.

This century, though, has brought many changes to Chinese opera. Performances today are commonly on Western-style stages with a curtain in front, painted scenery, electric lighting, sound amplification using body mikes, and subtitles projected on screens. (**Note:** The illustrations in this book, though accurately representing costume and makeup, are not meant to depict either traditional or modern stage settings.)

Mime and small props

Lacking scenery and almost any large props, traditional Chinese opera turned instead to the art of mime, often with handheld props to aid the illusion. A walk in a circle can mean a long journey. A tasseled whip can become a rider's horse. Several actors swaying together while one handles a paddle can portray a boat ride.

A table with chairs can become a sitting room, the emperor's court, or with a chair on top, a mountain to climb. A lantern in hand tells of night and darkness. A dance with blue flags means a flood, or with red ones, a fire. In such ways, Chinese opera portrays much that is not easily shown in realistic theater.

Dance, acrobatics, and other movement

While mime is one type of movement important in Chinese opera, another is dance. Some characters may dance almost constantly as they sing or speak. But even when actors aren't dancing, their steps and gestures are more or less stylized and dance-like. In fact, gesturing and even walking are considered arts in themselves.

One of the most popular features of Chinese opera is its acrobatics. All actors are trained in it, but it is the specialty of those who portray battle scenes. In these scenes, it is combined with stage fighting skills such as swordplay and kung fu.

This fighting, though, is stylized rather than realistic. No one dies onstage, and serious wounds are unlikely from spears tipped only with red ribbon. The attraction for the audience is not an illusion of violence but the incredible physical skills and interplay of the actors.

Costume

Chinese opera costumes are colorful, lavish, extravagant—a visual feast. Actors might wear richly embroidered coats, ceremonial robes, or full armor, along with elaborate headgear. Based loosely on fashions of several centuries ago, these costumes are not really meant to represent any historical period, or even to suggest a time of year. Instead they serve as pageantry and also to signal the character's age, social position, and personality.

Some costume elements are purely for show. For instance, young leading characters commonly wear "water sleeves"—lightweight white extensions of their regular sleeves that trail as low as the ground. These can flow gracefully at full length, or with a few flicks of the wrists fold back to expose the actor's hands. Warrior helmets are often graced by two pheasant feathers rising high, while armor is often augmented by four pennants jutting out from the back. Both additions create impressive effects during acrobatics.

Makeup

Among the most striking features of Chinese opera is the mask-like face painting of the "painted face" roles. The colors are bright—red, purple, black, white, blue, green, yellow—and are most often combined two or more in a complex pattern. As with costume, the purpose is both to appeal to the eye and to tell about the character. The colors represent strong personality traits—for instance, red for heroism, white for villainy. Some patterns identify particular characters or animals.

Most other actors make up their faces with white powder, plus rouge to highlight the mouth, eyes, and eyebrows. Male clowns announce themselves with a patch of white paint around the nose and eyes.

Music

The music in a Chinese opera is based on one or more standard melodies arranged to fit that opera. These melodies generally come from local musical tradition, and so will vary from one regional opera to another. Beijing Opera has drawn from a number of regional operas for its own large stock of melodies.

Traditionally, the music is played by six or seven musicians who sit in a back corner of the stage, in full view of the audience. Their instruments include traditional Chinese varieties of the fiddle, the banjo, the guitar, the flute, and the oboe, plus drums, gongs, cymbals, and a wooden clapper. The musicians interact closely with the actors, not only accompanying songs but also punctuating the action and the dialog with percussion, much as in an American circus.

Today, when a stage is Western-style, the musicians sit instead in the wing or in the orchestra pit. And their instruments might now include others from both China and the West—even an electric guitar!

For more about Chinese opera, you can read *Chinese Opera: Images and Stories*, by Peter Lovrick, photos by Siu Wang-Ngai, UBC Press, Vancouver, and University of Washington Press, Seattle, 1997; and *Peking Opera*, by Colin Mackerras, Oxford University Press, Hong Kong, 1997. Much on Chinese opera can be found by searching the World Wide Web. You might also look for Chinese opera videos at your library or at Web sites of Chinese video suppliers.

About the Story

The legend of White Snake is one of the most popular tales of China, with countless versions in folklore, literature, and drama. As a legend connected to Hangzhou's West Lake, it may have arisen as early as the seventh century. The thirteenth century saw the first literary versions, no doubt borrowed from professional storytellers in the streets of Hangzhou. It first appeared on stage in the fourteenth century, and the story is today one of the most often performed in Chinese opera.

This legend, though, has changed drastically from its beginnings. In the earliest versions, Lady White truly was a man-eating demon, and the Buddhist and Taoist priests who intervened were heroes. Over time she was portrayed more sympathetically, and popular sentiment came to side squarely with the lady and her quest for love. Nowadays in China, political interpretations are also common—but the story can be approached from many angles.

Though I consulted numerous versions of the legend, I based my retelling on the best-known and most influential one from modern Chinese opera, by the eminent author Tian Han. Two English translations of his libretto are *The White Snake: A Peking Opera*, by Tien Han, translated by Yang Hsien-yi and Gladys Yang, Foreign Languages Press, 1957; and *The White Snake*, by Tyan Han, translated by Donald Chang and William Packard, in *The Red Pear Garden: Three Great Dramas of Revolutionary China*, edited by John D. Mitchell, Godine, Boston, 1973. (Names here are as spelled in each book.) Though each translation has its strong points, the Yangs' is generally more readable and accurate.

Aaron Shepard

Here are some notes on important elements of the story. (Some earlier spellings are given in parentheses to help you recognize names in older books. But keep in mind that even the same spelling can take different forms—for instance, *Fahai, Fa Hai,* and *Fa-hai.*)

Hangzhou (Hangchow), West Lake, ¹Thunder Peak Pagoda, ²Broken Bridge. Hangzhou was China's illustrious capital in the twelfth and thirteenth centuries, when the White Snake legend had its greatest literary development. In fact, with over a million people, it was the largest, richest, and most culturally advanced city in the world. (Today it is a modern industrial city and one of China's busiest tourist spots.)

Just outside Hangzhou lies the wondrously lovely West Lake. This lake with its surrounding hills is a fairyland of lotuses, willows, peach and plum trees, pavilions, pagodas, temples, and ornamented boats. The White Snake legend came to be linked to Thunder Peak Pagoda, once the most prominent landmark of the south shore. The pagoda, though, collapsed in 1924—an event reflected in modern endings to the legend, like the one here.

Another landmark in the story, Broken Bridge, is still standing despite its name. There are several ideas about how it got that name, but we may never really know.

Zhenjiang (Chenchiang, Chinkiang), ³Gold Mountain Temple. Zhenjiang lies on the Yangzi (Yangtze) River and is connected to Hangzhou by the Grand Canal. Gold Mountain—actually a hill—was at the time of the story an island in the Yangzi, though the shifting river has now left it on the shore. There has been a combined temple and monastery there since around 400 A.D., and it may well have had a powerful abbot named Fahai.

Mount Emei (Omei), Kunlun (K'unlun) Mountain, Old Man of the South. Mount Emei lies in Sichuan (Sechuan, Szechwan) Province and is today a major site of Buddhist pilgrimage. Kunlun Mountain is more mythical, traditionally placed somewhere to the west, at the "center of the world." (On the map, the Kunlun Mountains are a major range on the north edge of the Tibetan Plateau—but their association with the mythical mountain is slight.)

Kunlun is said to be home to the most important Taoist goddess, the Queen Mother of the West, along with other gods and human Immortals. Among these gods is "The Old Man of the South," a nickname for the God of Longevity. He is in charge of the Star of Longevity—in Western terms, Canopus—in China's southern sky. The job of this god is to decide how long each person will live. In pictures, he is often shown with the "miracle mushroom" at his feet.

Chinese herbal medicine, miracle mushroom. Chinese herbal medicine still flourishes today, and herb shops much like Lady White's are found in Chinese communities worldwide. Hundreds of "herbs"—most taken from plants, but others from animals, insects, or minerals—are given singly or in combination, and in a variety of forms—teas, pills, powders, cakes, gels, tinctures, and ointments. Illnesses are diagnosed by several methods, including analyzing the pulse and examining the tongue.

"Miracle mushroom" is my own term for *lingzhi* (*lingchih, lingchi,* pronounced "LING-JEE"), known to Western scientists as *ganoderma lucidum.* It is a large woody mushroom that grows wild on decaying logs and stumps in coastal China. Once so rare and prized that it was used mostly by emperors, the mushroom is now cultivated commercially and sold worldwide, under those names and the Japanese *reishi* ("RAY-shee"). Herbalists recommend it for a wide variety of conditions, including AIDS and the side effects of chemotherapy.

Dragon Boat Festival, realgar wine. The Dragon Boat Festival, named after the colorful boat races on that day, is one of the three most important holidays of the Chinese year. It falls on the fifth day of the fifth lunar month—about the first week of June. The festival is said to commemorate the death of Qu Yuan ("CHOO yoo-ON"), an ancient poet and royal adviser, though it likely started earlier as a solstice celebration. Because of the festival's place in the White Snake legend, the story is often told or performed at this time.

Formerly, it was the custom during the festival to drink wine mixed with realgar—arsenic sulfide—in the belief that the foul odor repelled snakes. These and other poisonous animals are at their most troublesome at this hot time of year, and the festival day is considered especially unlucky in this regard. Nowadays realgar wine is rarely drunk but may still be rubbed on the skin.

A. S.